# This CROWN

Ashley Sewell

illustrated by Max Rambaldi

AuthorHouse™
1663 Liberty Drive
Bloomington, IN 47403
www.authorhouse.com
Phone: 1 (800) 839-8640

Because of the dynamic nature of the Internet, any web addresses or links contained in
this book may have changed since publication and may no longer be valid. The views
expressed in this work are solely those of the author and do not necessarily reflect the views
of the publisher, and the publisher hereby disclaims any responsibility for them.

Any people depicted in stock imagery provided by Getty Images are models,
and such images are being used for illustrative purposes only.
Certain stock imagery © Getty Images.

This book is printed on acid-free paper.

ISBN: 978-1-7283-5028-8 (hc)
ISBN: 978-1-7283-3667-1 (sc)
ISBN: 978-1-7283-3668-8 (e)

Library of Congress Control Number: 2019919674

Print information available on the last page.

Published by AuthorHouse 12/04/2019

authorHOUSE®

# Dedication

For Jordyn and Jules— such vibrant rays of light who embody what it means to be "beautiful, bold, and smart."

For all of the queens, of all ages, that I have been blessed to know and love; both here with us on earth, and those who have gone to their heavenly home. Your magic serves as a constant inspiration.

For my mother who has always taught me what it means to be a queen.

You are a queen!
Do you know
what that means?

You are beautiful,
bold, and smart.

One of God's
most precious
works of art.

From your thick
natural hair,
to your dancing toes,

4

You glow, girl!
And everybody knows.

5

You are a queen!
Do you know
what that means?

You can do anything
that you set your mind to.

Just remember to
always be true.

And if you want to make
a difference in this world,

keep in mind,
it starts with you.

So, speak
your mind,
all the time!

Reach out!
Take risks!

And don't be afraid to be different.

You are a queen,
do you know
what that means?

You can dream,
you can fly,

And remember,
my queen,
it's ok to cry.

When times
get rough,
and you feel like
you've had enough,

Believe in yourself.
Don't ever give up!

You are a queen!
Do you know
what that means?

One day,
you might find your king.

He's only your king
if he treats you with respect,
And queens do not settle
for anything less!

18

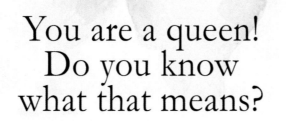

You are a queen!
Do you know
what that means?

Yes I do.

It means I am strong, I am proud,
I will walk through this life
with my head held high,

And never let anyone
bring it down.

21

Because I am a queen!

And I know that I'm worthy
of wearing this crown.

# Acknowledgements

I'd like to acknowledge all of my family; my village. Special thanks to Erik for believing in me, Michelle for encouraging me to complete and publish this project, and everyone who provided feedback when I shared pieces of this work with you before publishing. Much love to you all.

# About the Author

Ashley Sewell is an educator who was born in Seattle, WA, and raised in Oakland, CA, where she currently resides. She has a Master of Education in Urban Education, a Multiple Subject Teaching Credential, and a Bachelor of Arts in Psychology and Behavioral Science. She has always been dedicated to uplifting and empowering youth, and this book is a product of that goal. In her free time, she enjoys spending quality time with family and friends, creating and enjoying art, and traveling.

Printed in the United States
By Bookmasters